overheard
at
whole foods

quotes overheard in public

and transcribed by

nathan bragg

theresa vogrin

idiocratea

Copyright © 2019 Idiocratea

Art Direction and Cover Design by Nathan Bragg

Illustrations by Theresa Vogrin

All rights reserved. No part of this book may be used, performed or reproduced in any form or by any electronic or mechanical means, including photocopying and recording, or by any information storage and retrieval system, without prior written consent from the author except for brief quotations in critical articles or reviews.

Idiocratea is an imprint of Polygon Publishing LTD.

POLYGON PUBLISHING

www.polygonpublishing.com

www.idiocratea.com

ISBN-13: 978-1798036259

This book is not authorized, endorsed by or affiliated with *Whole Foods* or its subsidiaries.

*this book
is for
all whole foods customers
who brighten up our days
with their heartfelt
complaints
concerns
statements.*

*keep calm
and
carry on
shopping.*

contents

the gossiping 7

the loving 41

the pestering 77

the
gossiping

overheard at whole foods

it smells
like white people
and la croix in here.

overheard at whole foods

seriously laura
after he cheated on me
i feel like nothing is real.

like is that milk even organic?

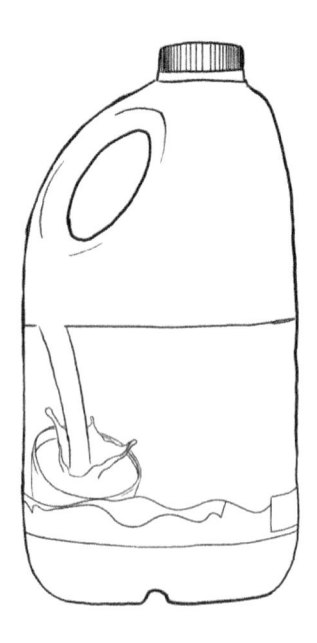

overheard at whole foods

some people think
i'm crazy
for suggesting this
but why don't we put dogs
on treadmills to
generate electricity?

they love to run.

overheard at whole foods

i found
the most perfect house
but there is
no whole foods nearby
so i'm still looking.

overheard at whole foods

we basically made piña colada
but instead of rum
we put in kale.

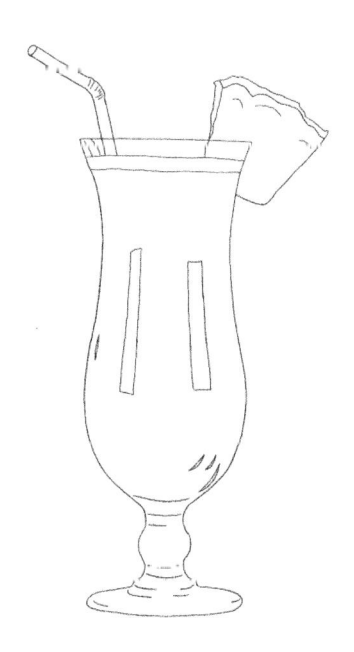

overheard at whole foods

yoga helps you
look and feel
better naked.

                                              so does tequila.

overheard at whole foods

my doctor says
my intestines are
too long
so i'll have to
give up gluten.

you don't want that.
it has dairy.

that's like liquid meat.

overheard at whole foods

i've been drinking
a lot of bottled water
and i'm too scared
to drink tap water now
because i don't want
a reverse reaction.

overheard at whole foods

don't buy that batch of kale.
buy this one.
its aura is stronger.

overheard at whole foods

look
she's paying
in cash.
that's so cool.

overheard at whole foods

my dog
recently started
the 30-day vegan challenge.

overheard at whole foods

oh no
i'm not fussy at all.

i'll eat anything
as long as it is
gluten-free
dairy-free
low-carb
low-fat
low-calorie
sugar-free
unprocessed
fair trade
raw
and organic.

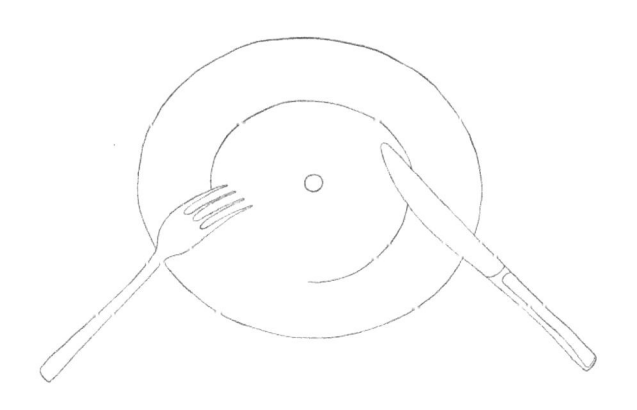

overheard at whole foods

ew
there are raisins
in my quinoa salad.

                          are they raisins
                      or just really plump
                            goji berries?

oh never mind.
goji.
all clear.

overheard at whole foods

beer
isn't on my cleanse.

>it's hops juice.
you're fine.

overheard at whole foods

i really needed
to come in
and get a kombucha.

i'm having a very emotional day.

somebody must have
accidentally eaten gluten.

- guy staring at ambulance in front of whole foods

overheard at whole foods

farro
is totally
the new quinoa.

overheard at whole foods

i was really attracted
to this guy in yoga class
but there was something
about his downward dog
that said *married.*

overheard at whole foods

people are screaming
for their freedom
in the ukraine.

here they're screaming
for more tomatoes
at the salad bar.

overheard at whole foods

i mean
i don't hate her at all.
i don't hate people.

but i would like
to see her
catch on fire
in agony once or twice.

overheard at whole foods

taking pictures
of your food
as it arrives
is the new way
of saying grace.

unless you're verified
on social media
don't call yourself
a public figure.

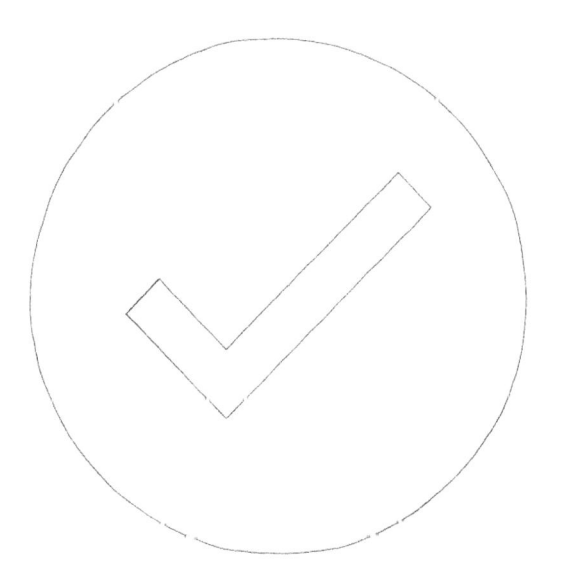

overheard at whole foods

getting carded
to buy kombucha
makes me feel
like a better class
of alcoholic.

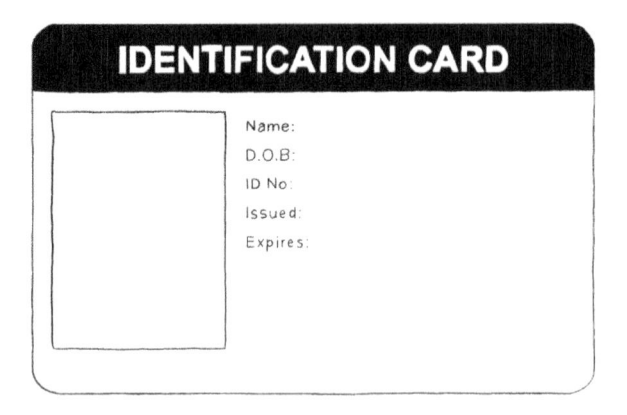

IDENTIFICATION CARD

Name:
D.O.B:
ID No:
Issued:
Expires:

overheard at whole foods

oh my gosh
this is my third
gluten free coffee today.

i'm totally addicted.

overheard at whole foods

stop going on and on
about your diet.

just eat your salad
and be sad.

overheard at whole foods

i don't know
if i believe
in this horoscope thing
because i read friday's
and it says
i'm going to die.

she moved to hawaii
to have her baby
with dolphins.

apparently
they kiss your baby
as it comes out
and it gives it
a kundalini awakening.

i'm a raw vegan
but i'm still eating
chicken and fish.

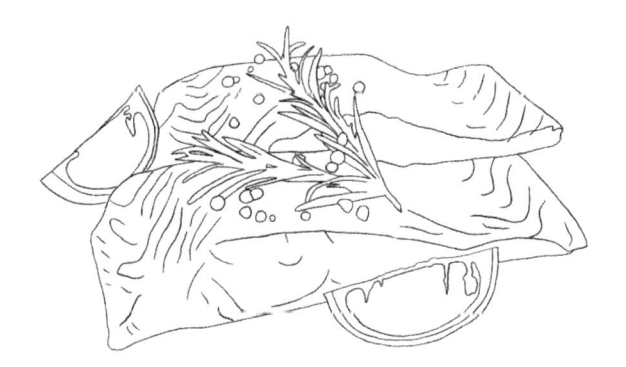

oh yes.
i can feel it
exploding open
my crown chakra.

- *woman tasting root beer*

overheard at whole foods

she's a witch
in training.

she's been
reading crystals
since she was 2.

she's 8 now.

the
loving

overheard at whole foods

what kind of choices
do you want to make
in life isaac?
good or bad?
mango or banana?

- *dad to son*

overheard at whole foods

look momma in the eye.
we are going
into the wine section.
momma needs her juice.

i bought you a coconut water
so will you be still?
look momma in the eye.
say yes momma.

overheard at whole foods

mommy just needs to grab
some kale chips
and almond milk.

then we can get food
at mcdonald's.

overheard at whole foods

stop it now
or i'll have to put
your sushi back.

- *mother to annoying child*

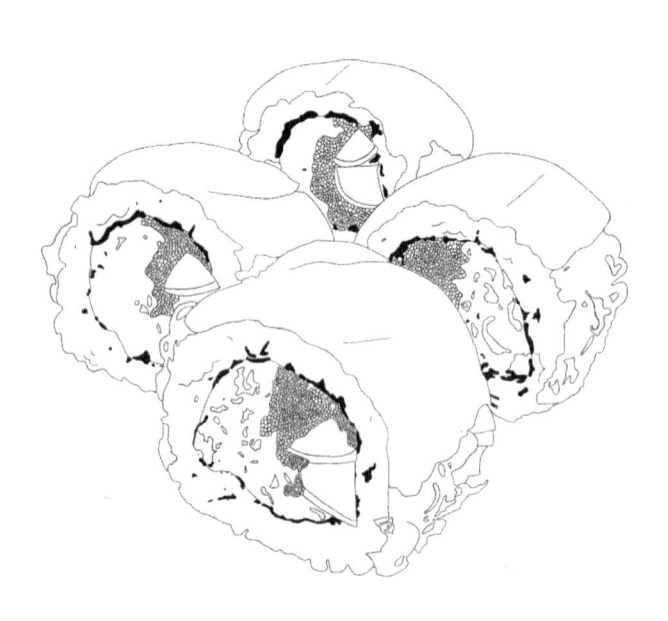

overheard at whole foods

they are not fish fingers
phoebe.

they are
lemon sole goujons.

overheard at whole foods

make sure
you get daddy an ipa.

- *girl to mother in beer aisle*

these strawberries
are really nice.

>*nice* is such a bland word.
>can't you use something
>a little more descriptive
>darling?

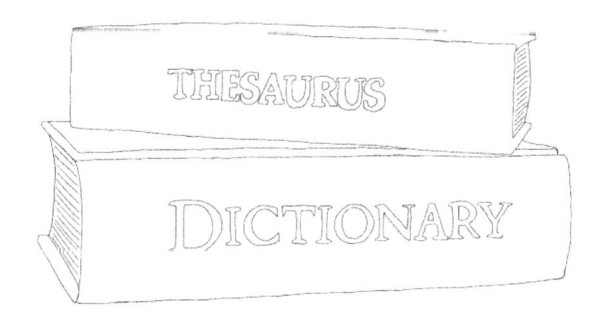

overheard at whole foods

here is an expression
mommy would be happy
for you to learn.
fair trade.

- *mother to her toddler*

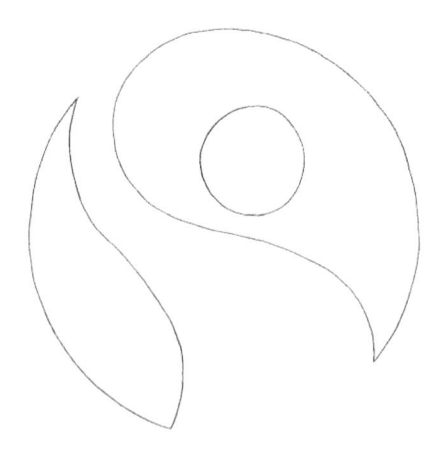

overheard at whole foods

i'm not buying
an organic cucumber
for your guinea pig.

i love him
but i don't love him
that much.

overheard at whole foods

mommy
are we spending christmas
on the boat this year?

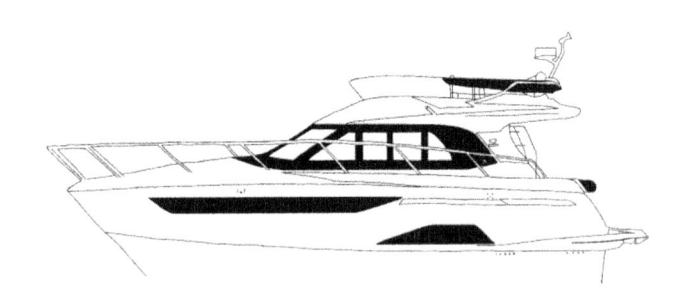

darling
they've changed
the packaging
on those beans.

i can't buy them now.
they won't look so nice
in the cupboard.

overheard at whole foods

where does milk
come from?

                                        almonds.

- nanny and toddler

overheard at whole foods

you've got
poppy seeds
in your teeth.

                                        they aren't
                                    poppy seeds
                               they're chia seeds.

whatever
you should floss more.

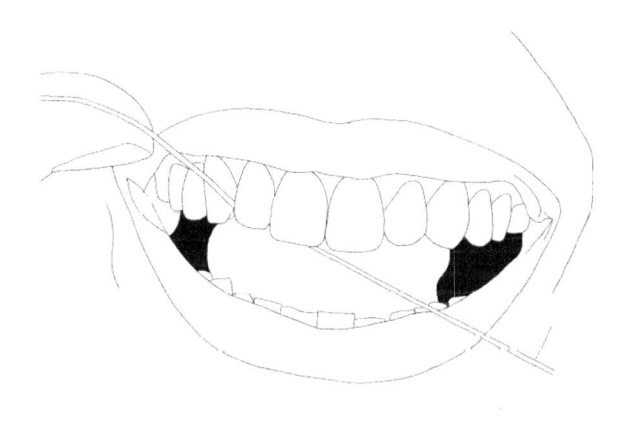

overheard at whole foods

hey honey
can you make sure
to record that special
on the amish tonight?

- *man on his phone in the check-out line*

overheard at whole foods

darling
what are we going to do?

they're out of
the spanish goat cheese
and the dog won't eat
any other kind.

overheard at whole foods

if it's not organic
i'm not eating it.

it's rather quite simple
when you think about it
mommy.

- *little girl to her mother*

can we
break up
somewhere else?

this is
my favorite
whole foods store.

overheard at whole foods

can i scream
for 30 seconds?
i'll do extra reading.

                                                no
                                   i said you could
                               either have a crêpe
                                      or scream.

- child and mother

just pick one.

> i can't.
> i need to figure out
> which one will be
> the healthiest
> and most beneficial
> and there are so many
> and it is so hard.

it's just water.

overheard at whole foods

put that back
darling.
we only buy
twice pressed olive oil.

overheard at whole foods

come on julian
surely you recognize this wine?
you've been to the chateau.

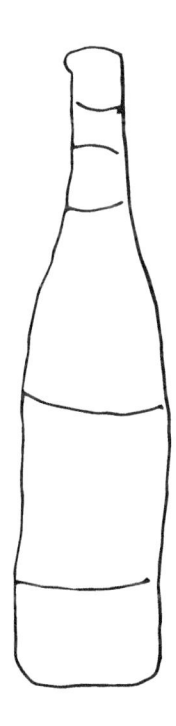

overheard at whole foods

i hate
that they are always
asking me
to donate to charity
at the check-out.

if i wanted a guilt trip
i would have gone shopping
with my mother.

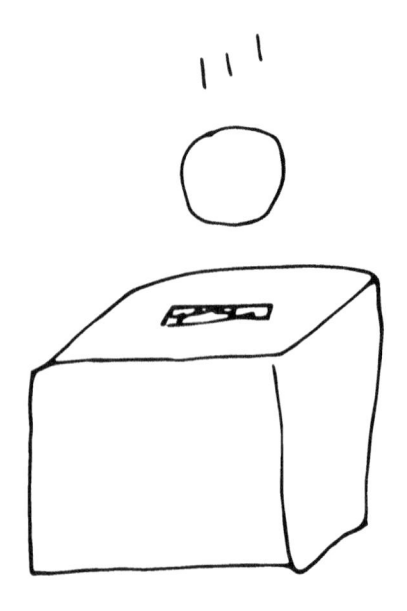

honey
when i die
just shower my grave
in fair trade
organic
chocolate covered
almonds.

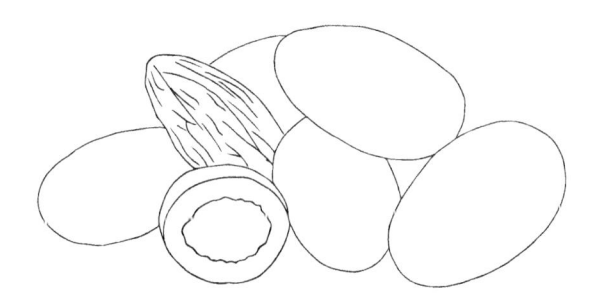

overheard at whole foods

mom
what's apple cider vinegar?

i think
it's like kombucha.

overheard at whole foods

should we get
an emergency stilton?

overheard at whole foods

mom
everyone at school says
you don't love me.
they laugh at me
because my fruit
isn't organic.

overheard at whole foods

these bananas are
from saint lucia.
we holidayed there
last year.

overheard at whole foods

babe
we don't need
anything else.

we have so much food
we could feed
a vegan army.

overheard at whole foods

did you see
my dog's instagram account
today?

                                                no
                              what did i miss?

it was his birthday
and we made a special hat
and outfit for him
and threw him a birthday party.
you'll have to check out
the pictures.

overheard at whole foods

no it's not
mousakaaa.

it's mous-a-ka.

overheard at whole foods

we can only bake
gluten free cookies
for santa
honey.

- *lady to toddler*

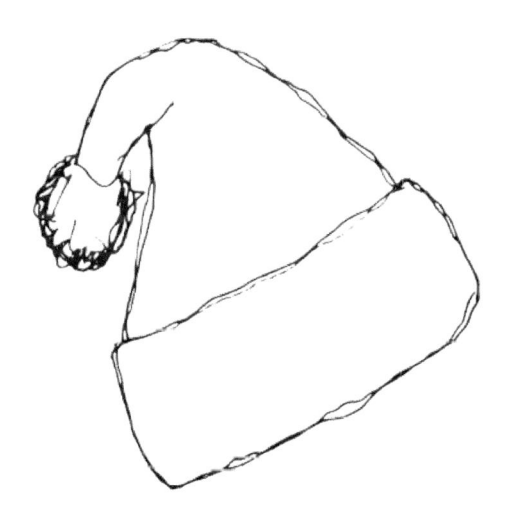

overheard at whole foods

if you insist on
egging mr. robertson's house
at least use quail eggs.

overheard at whole foods

oh no
the lemon chesapeake
is gone.
it's my favorite.

                                      just order it online
                                                honey.

the pestering

overheard at whole foods

do you carry
long pumpkin?

> i'm not sure
> what that is?

ugh.
sometimes
they are called zucchini.

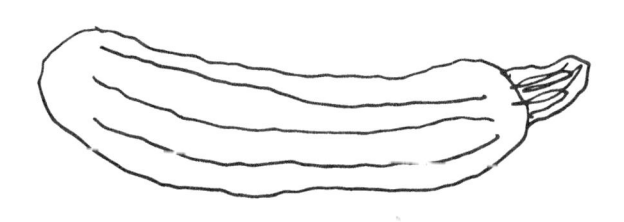

excuse me
do you have
grass fed salmon?

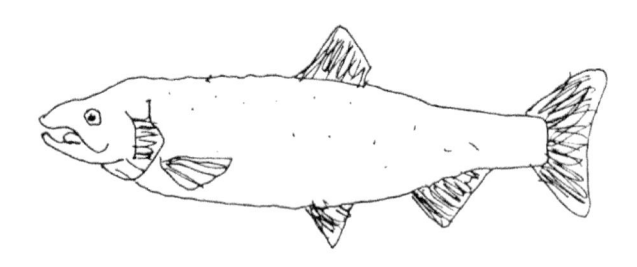

overheard at whole foods

i need some
artisan meats
for my artisan bread.

overheard at whole foods

i heard
that some mushrooms
are poisonous.

is your
creamy mushroom soup
made with those ones
or another kind?

overheard at whole foods

excuse me?
i need to change
my holiday order.

i forgot that my 5-year-old
doesn't like rib roast.
he only eats filet mignon.

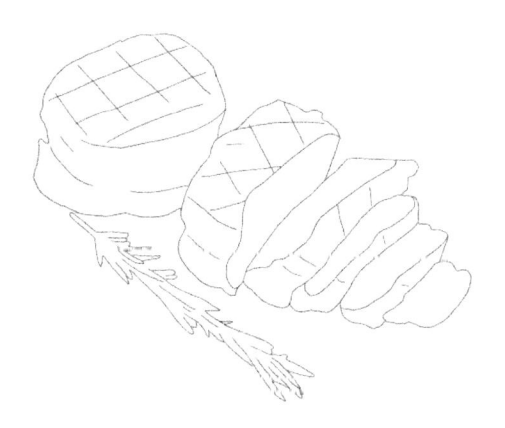

overheard at whole foods

tell your manager
to put the mayonnaise
on sale.
this one right here.

overheard at whole foods

excuse me
would you smell
my face?

i just put
some face cream on
and i want to know
if my husband will notice.

- *customer to employee*

why don't you
have pancetta?

i'll have to make
my pasta sauce
with canadian bacon now.

overheard at whole foods

what?
you don't sell
camel milk?

overheard at whole foods

just tell me
where i can find kale chips.
is that too much to ask?

overheard at whole foods

do you have
a soy-based
non-diary substitute
for heavy cream?

overheard at whole foods

will you serve
my mocha
before i have to leave?

- after the fire alarm went off

overheard at whole foods

is there any way
i can order
a vegan
sugar free cupcake?
it's for
my dog's birthday.

excuse me
the coffee machine
is broken.

                                                      you can still get
                                                        coffee and tea
                                                               from it
                                                     just not a latte
                                                   or cappuccino.

so the coffee machine
is broken.

overheard at whole foods

how can you be
out of vegan parfaits?

are you going
to go out to my car
and tell my daughter
that you are
out of vegan parfaits?

overheard at whole foods

i need to read
the numbers
on the barcode
aloud to you.

i don't want any lasers
touching my food.

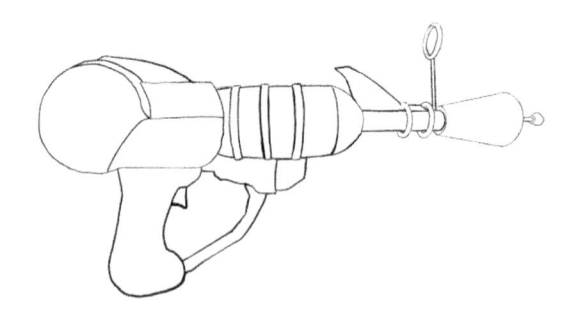

overheard at whole foods

technically
vegetables are not vegan
because you need to fertilize them
with animal manure.

overheard at whole foods

what's in
your dog cakes?

                              unbleached organic flour.

oh right.
my dog is gluten free.

overheard at whole foods

listen
we have
a real emergency.
we are out of vegan doughnuts
in the front.

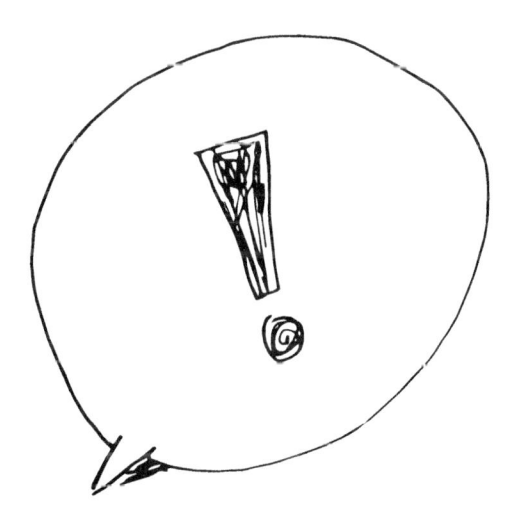

i wish
whole foods sold
organic cocaine.

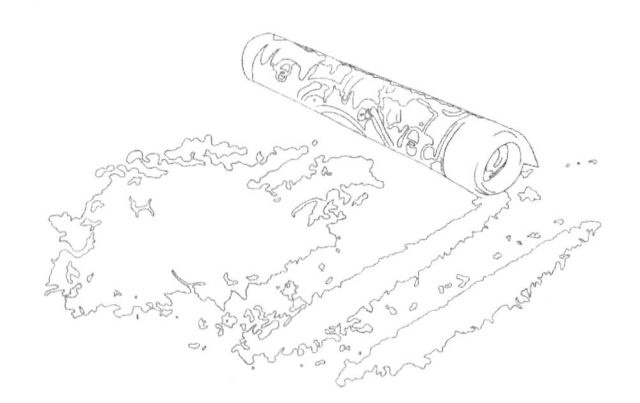

if you enjoyed *overheard at whole foods*
please consider leaving a review
on amazon.

thank you.

other books published by *idiocratea*:

overheard at waitrose
overheard at waitrose II
google search poetry
milk and brexit

about this book

overheard at whole foods is a collection of the most iconic quotes overheard in *whole foods* stores and posted across social media platforms like twitter, facebook and instagram under the meme name *overheard in whole foods*.

idiocratea doesn't hold the copyright to the words, only to the illustrations and the presentation of the quotes.

our only intention with this book is to make people laugh and brighten up their day.

about *idiocratea*

idiocratea is an imprint of Polygon Publishing LTD. with our constantly expanding selection of trendy mugs, meme related products, gag gifts, personalised items and our very own range of original books, we at *idiocratea* pride ourselves on selling extraordinary gifts for extraordinary people.

check us out on instagram (@idiocratea_ and @polygon.publishing) and don't forget to browse our stores at **www.idiocratea.com** and **www.polygonpublishing.com**.

about the contributors

nathan bragg

nathan bragg is a uk-based digital marketing specialist, entrepreneur and lover of memes.

theresa vogrin

theresa vogrin is an austrian writer, living in the uk. she published her debut poetry book *Bitter-Sweet* in july 2018.

check out theresa's work on instagram (@theresa_vogrin) and facebook.